STAND UP  SPEAK OUT

EDUCATION ACTIVISM

Virginia Loh-Hagan

45TH PARALLEL PRESS

Published in the United States of America by Cherry Lake Publishing Group
Ann Arbor, Michigan
www.cherrylakepublishing.com

Reading Adviser: Beth Walker Gambro, MS, Ed., Reading Consultant, Yorkville, IL
Book Designer: Jen Wahi

Photo Credits: © Eugenio Marongiu/Shutterstock.com, 4; © milatas/Shutterstock.com, 6; © A M Syed/Shutterstock.com, 8; © Avatar_023/Shutterstock.com, 11; © Asier Romero/Shutterstock.com, 12; © wavebreakmedia/Shutterstock.com, 14; © FatCamera/iStock.com, 17; © Mangkorn Danggura/Shutterstock.com, 18; © Indian Food Images/Shutterstock.com, 20; © addkm/Shutterstock.com, 23; © TB studio/Shutterstock.com, 24; © Hayk_Shalunts/Shutterstock.com, 26; © Rob Crandall/Shutterstock.com, 29; © ROM_images/Shutterstock.com, 30, additional cover images courtesy of iStock.com

45th Parallel Press is an imprint of Cherry Lake Publishing Group.

Library of Congress Cataloging-in-Publication Data

Names: Loh-Hagan, Virginia, author.
Title: Education activism/ Virginia Loh-Hagan.
Description: Ann Arbor, Michigan : Cherry Lake Publishing, [2021] | Series: Stand up, speak out | Includes index.
Identifiers: LCCN 2021004983 (print) | LCCN 2021004984 (ebook) | ISBN 9781534187566 (hardcover) | ISBN 9781534188969 (paperback) | ISBN 9781534190368 (pdf) | ISBN 9781534191761 (ebook)
Subjects: LCSH: Student movements–Juvenile literature. | Students–Political activity–Juvenile literature. | Educational change–Juvenile literature.
Classification: LCC LB3610 .L65 2021 (print) | LCC LB3610 (ebook) | DDC 371.8/1–dc23
LC record available at https://lccn.loc.gov/2021004983
LC ebook record available at https://lccn.loc.gov/2021004984

Printed in the United States of America
Corporate Graphics

About the Author:

Dr. Virginia Loh-Hagan is an author, university professor, and former classroom teacher. She's currently the Director of the Asian Pacific Islander Desi American Resource Center at San Diego State University. She's worked in education for more than 20 years. She lives in San Diego with her very tall husband and very naughty dogs.

TABLE OF CONTENTS

Activists often work as a group. They have power in numbers.

WHAT IS EDUCATION ACTIVISM?

Everyone has the power to make our world a better place. A person just has to act. **Activists** fight for change. They fight for their beliefs. They see unfair things. They want to correct wrongs. They want **justice**. Justice is upholding what is right. Activists help others. They serve people and communities.

There are many problems in the world. Activists seek to solve these problems. They learn all they can. They raise awareness. They take action. They inspire others to act.

Activists care very deeply about their **causes**. Causes are principles, aims, or movements. They give rise to activism.

Many activists feel strongly about education rights. They believe all children have the right to a free public education. But that isn't always the case. Not all children can go to school. Some are **discriminated** against. Discriminate means to treat unfairly due to things such as sex, race, age, or religion.

Some children are denied access to schools. Some are not given the same opportunities as others. Some do not feel safe in schools.

In this book, we share examples of education rights issues and actions. We also share tips for how to engage. Your activist journey starts here!

● Education programs around the world are different.

GET STARTED

Community service is about helping others. It's about creating a kinder world. Activism goes beyond service. It's about making a fairer and more just world. It involves acting and fighting for change. Choose to be an activist!

- **Focus on your cause!** In addition to the topics covered in this book, there are many others. Other examples include working to end the school-to-prison pipeline and including all voices in school materials.

- **Do your research!** Learn all you can about the cause. Learn about the history. Learn from other activists.

- **Make a plan!** Get organized.

- **Make it happen!** Act! There are many ways to act. Activists write letters. They write petitions. They protest. They march in the streets. They ban or **boycott**. Boycott means to avoid or not buy something as a protest. They perform art to make people aware. They post to social media. They fight to change laws. They organize sit-in events. They participate in demonstrations and **strikes**. During strikes, people protest by refusing to do something, such as work.

More than 132 million girls around the world are not in school.

CHAPTER 1

FIGHT FOR GIRLS' EDUCATION

Around the world, girls are denied education. They're forced to marry early. They're forced to work. They're seen as less smart than boys. This is wrong. Girls deserve the chance to go to school. When girls go to school, communities improve.

Malala Yousafzai is from Pakistan. She was denied an education. She fought back. At age 11, she blogged about the injustices. In 2012, she was going home from school. She was shot in the head. She survived. She speaks out for girls' rights. She makes speeches and writes books. At age 17, she won a Nobel Peace Prize. She's the youngest person to do so.

Zuriel Oduwole was born in California. Her father was from Nigeria. Her mother was from Mauritius. At age 9,

GET INSPIRED

BY PIONEERS IN EDUCATION ACTIVISM!

○ **Horace Mann** shaped American public schools. In 1837, he became Massachusetts' first Secretary of Education. He made sure every child could have a free public education. He funded the schools with local taxes. He also helped develop teacher training schools. He supported free public libraries.

○ **Booker T. Washington** was born into slavery. He helped African Americans get access to education. In 1881, he led Tuskegee University. Tuskegee is a historically Black university. Washington was the first African American to be invited to the White House.

○ **Maria Montessori** was one of the first female Italian doctors. She had enrolled in an all-male school. She studied how young children learned. She changed how people taught early education. She believed young children were creative. In 1907, she started her first school in Rome. She wrote many books. She inspired Montessori schools around the world.

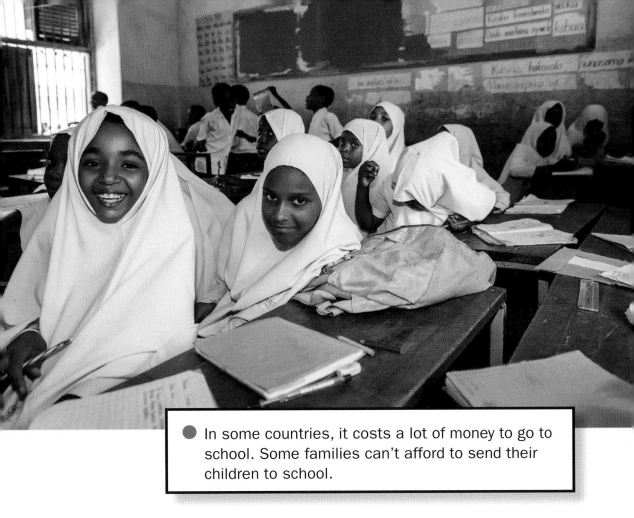

In some countries, it costs a lot of money to go to school. Some families can't afford to send their children to school.

Zuriel went to Ghana. She was surprised by how many girls weren't in school. At age 12, she made a film about Ghana. She became one of the world's youngest filmmakers. She made more films. In 2013, she founded "Dream Up, Speak Up, Stand Up." She encourages African girls to get an education. She speaks out against child marriage.

She fights to remove barriers to education for girls. She's

● October 11 is International Day of the Girl. It celebrates girls' accomplishments. It also promotes gender equality.

met with more than 30 world leaders. She's been on TV shows.

Michelle Obama was the First Lady of the United States from 2009 to 2017. She launched Let Girls Learn. She gives money. She supports programs that support girls' education.

Stand Up, Speak Out

In some developing countries, girls lack access to sanitary products. This means they have to miss school when they have menstrual periods. When girls are forced to miss school, they are more likely to drop out. In India, 1 in 5 girls drop out of school after they get their period. Without an education, most girls end up in poverty. This is called period poverty. Activists want girls to go to school. You can help!

 Research organizations that help combat period poverty. Donate sanitary products to these organizations and homeless shelters.

Learn about activist groups supporting girls' education. Invite speakers to come talk at your school. Let people know about these issues.

Raise funds to help activist groups. There are lots of ways to raise money. Host fun runs. Host bake sales.

● Inclusive education means serving all students in the same classroom.

SUPPORT INCLUSIVE CLASSROOMS

Some students have disabilities. Some aren't treated fairly in schools. They're ignored. They don't get a high-quality education.

Mosharraf Hossain is from Bangladesh in Asia. Hossain started an activist group. His group wants to change how people think about people with disabilities. Only 10 percent of Bangladeshi children with disabilities are in schools. Some students with disabilities are separated from other students. They get low-quality education. Hossain's group works with teachers to create **inclusive** programs. Inclusive means open to all.

GET INSPIRED

BY LEGAL VICTORIES

○ Linda Brown wasn't allowed to go to an all-White school. Her father, Oliver Brown, sued the state of Kansas. He said schools for Black children weren't equal to the White schools. Black schools had less money. Most didn't have cafeterias, libraries, or gyms. Some didn't have running water or electricity. In 1954, *Brown v. Board of Education* ended race **segregation** in schools. Segregation means keeping apart. Many schools protested. Activists had to keep fighting to integrate schools.

○ Boyd County High School is in Kentucky. In 2002, students wanted to form a Gay-Straight **Alliance** (GSA) club. Alliance means group. The school approved it at first. Then, people protested against the club. The school shut down all student clubs. But the Bible club and drama club still met at the school. The GSA students thought this was unfair. They sued and won. The school was required to treat all students equally.

In 1960, U.S. parents fought for their children with disabilities. In 1975, a law passed. It gave children the right to public education. Activists fought for improvements. In 1990, the law became the Individuals with Disabilities Act (IDEA). Judith Heumann worked on this law.

Heumann uses a wheelchair. Her mother fought for her to go to school. Heumann became a disability rights activist.

The IDEA law requires schools to make sure students with disabilities are not punished at rates higher than their peers.

She became the first wheelchair user to teach in New York City. She fought for ramps. She fought for student rights. She hosted protests. She organized a sit-in at a government building in San Francisco, California. More than 150 people participated. The sit-in lasted 28 days. It was the longest sit-in at a government building.

● It's important to have highly trained teachers. Teachers who work with students with disabilities are called Intervention Specialists.

Stand Up, Speak Out

Ableism is discrimination against people with disabilities. Be a friend. Be kind. Activists want people to be **allies**. Allies are supporters. You can help!

> Use "people first" language. Say "a person with a disability." Don't say a "disabled person." Don't use words that put down people.

> Don't make jokes about people with disabilities. Stop others from making jokes. Call them out. Tell them to be better.

> Write to politicians. Support laws that serve people with disabilities.

In other countries, students have a longer time to eat lunch. So, they go home for lunch.

CHAPTER 3

IMPROVE SCHOOL FOOD

In the United States, child **obesity** has increased. Obesity refers to a body weight that is above healthy. People worry about children's health. Most children eat school food. Activists work to improve school lunches. They promote healthy eating.

Andrea Strong is a mom in New York. In 2018, she founded the NYC Healthy School Food Alliance. Strong hosts rallies and marches. She organizes petitions. She encourages families to eat home-cooked meals. She believes in health education and gardens in schools. She wants students to have more time to eat lunch. She says students need more recess time for exercise.

GET IN THE KNOW

KNOW THE HISTORY

○ **1734** Anton Wilhelm Amo was from Ghana. He was enslaved. He was bought by German dukes. He was sent to German schools. He became the first African to get a doctorate degree.

○ **1792** Mary Wollstonecraft was a British women's rights advocate. She published *A Vindication of the Rights of Woman*. It examined men and women. She argued men and women were equal except in education. She thought women should also be educated. She said that children should be sent to free day schools. Her ideas were considered extreme at the time.

○ **1885** Mamie Tape was a Chinese American girl. She was denied access to an all-White school. Her mother, Mary Tape, fought back. She wrote a letter to school officials. She went to court. The court ruled in her favor. It said that schools couldn't exclude Chinese Americans.

○ **1950** About 20,000 New York City high school students walked out of class. They did this for 3 days. They wanted the mayor to give teachers pay raises.

Bettina Elias Seigel is a mom. She writes a blog. Her blog is called "The Lunch Tray." Seigel wants to improve school lunches. She creates online petitions. She encouraged schools to buy healthier ground meat.

In 2010, the U.S. Congress passed the Healthy Hunger-Free Kids Act. The law made schools serve more fruits and vegetables. It increased whole-grain foods. It limited fat and salt. It limited meats. The meals are healthier. But some students say they're still hungry. Wallace High School students made a YouTube video about the reduced size of school lunches. They got more than 1.5 million views. Other students spoke out as well.

● Some activists host workshops on healthy eating habits.

Stand Up, Speak Out

Some students go hungry. They don't have enough food. The only meal they get may be at school. They don't know when they'll get their next meal. This is called food **insecurity**. Insecurity means not knowing. Activists want to end food insecurity. You can help!

> Create a food **pantry**. A pantry is a small space that stores food. Collect food donations. Store it in the pantry. Let people take food when they need it.

> Start a community garden. Grow vegetables to make salads and other healthy dishes. Teach people how to garden. Let people use the garden whenever they need food.

> Write to school officials. Ask them to provide more free meals.

Don't name the shooter. Don't make them famous. Focus on the victims.

CHAPTER 4

STOP SCHOOL SHOOTINGS

Students should feel safe in schools. But gun violence has changed this. Schools have been targeted. One school shooting is one too many.

In 2015, there was a shooting in Kenya in Africa. Gunmen attacked Garissa University. They attacked during morning prayers. They killed at least 148 people, mostly students. They hurt about 80 people. They took students as **hostages**. Hostages are people held as prisoners. More than 500 students escaped. Ory Okolloh is a Kenyan activist. She started a social media project. She asked people to post pictures of the victims. She said, "We will name them. One by one." She wanted to honor each victim.

GET INVOLVED

There are several groups working to protect education rights. Connect with them to get more involved.

- **CAMFED** is the Campaign for Female Education. Group members fight for girls to be educated in Africa. They want girls to be leaders. They want girls to have options in life.

- **Dolly Parton's Imagination Library** gives free books to young children.

- **Girls Who Code** supports women in science and math jobs. The group provides free computer science classes. It provides summer camps. It wants men and women to have the same opportunities.

- **NEA** is the National Education Association. This group fights for public education. It has more than 3 million members. They help create laws and policies.

- **Sound Out** promotes student voices. Group members focus on teaching students how to improve schools. They work with school partners and provide resources.

In 2018, a gunman opened fire at Marjory Stoneman Douglas (MSD) High School in Parkland, Florida. The gunman killed 17 people and hurt another 17 people. Parkland student survivors formed an activist group called Never Again MSD. They fight to reform gun laws. They fight for gun safety.

Emma Gonzalez is a Parkland survivor. She said,

About 1.2 million people participated in the March for Our Lives around the United States.

"We are going to be the last mass shooting."
She helped organize the March for Our Lives. The
march supported gun control laws.

Florida passed a law called the MSD Public Safety
Act. The Florida governor said to the students, "You
made your voices heard. You didn't let up and you
fought until there was change."

In 2018, the March for Our Lives
organization traveled the country.
They registered more than 50,000
new voters.

Stand Up, Speak Out

To stop school shootings, we can do more than focus on guns. We can focus on social and emotional health. We can improve school environments. We can better support at-risk children.

 Talk to school leaders. Ask for more wellness programs. Ask for more mental health support. Ask for more counselors.

 Start an anti-bullying program. Call people out for bullying.

 Stay alert. Listen to each other. Be aware of threats. If people talk about killing or guns, take it seriously. Report any problems to adults.

GLOSSARY

ableism (AY-buh-lih-zuhm) discrimination against people with special needs

activists (AK-tih-vists) people who fight for political or social change

alliance (uh-LYE-uhnss) a united group focused on a cause or goal

allies (AL-eyes) supporters

boycott (BOI-kot) to refuse to buy something or take part in something as a protest to force change

causes (KAWZ-es) the reasons for activism

discriminated (diss-krim-uh-NAY-tuhd) have treated someone unfairly because of their sex, race, age, or religion

hostages (HOSS-tij-es) people being held as security for the fulfillment of a condition

inclusive (in-KLOO-siv) being open to all

insecurity (in-sih-KYOOR-uh-tee) being not sure of something

justice (JUHSS-tiss) the upholding of what is fair and right

obesity (oh-BEE-suh-tee) the condition of being unhealthily overweight

pantry (PAN-tree) a small area to store food

segregation (seg-ruh-GAY-shuhn) kept apart

strikes (STRYKES) organized protests where people refuse to do something

LEARN MORE!

Brown, Dinah. *Who Is Malala Yousafzai?* New York, NY: Penguin Young Readers Group, 2015.

Tonatiuh, Duncan. *Separate Is Never Equal*: *Sylvia Mendez and Her Family's Fight for Desegregation*. New York, NY: Abrams Books, 2014.

Tougas, Shelley. *Little Rock Girl 1957*: *How a Photograph Changed the Fight for Integration*. Mankato, MN: Compass Point Books, 2012.

INDEX